DOES GOD
ANSWER PRAYER?

DOES GOD ANSWER PRAYER?

PETER BAELZ

TEMPLEGATE PUBLISHERS
SPRINGFIELD, ILLINOIS

© Peter Baelz 1983

Made and published in the United States by
Templegate Publishers
302 East Adams Street
P.O. Box 5152
Springfield, Illinois 62705

ISBN 0-87243-117-7

7053453

Acknowledgement

The majority of Scripture quotations in this
publication are from the Revised Standard
Version of the Bible, copyrighted 1971 and
1952 by the Division of Christian Education
of the National Council of the Churches of
Christ in the USA.

CONTENTS

The best prayer is to rest in the goodness
of God knowing that that goodness can reach
right down to our lowest depths of need.

Julian of Norwich

I.
POWER OR PRESENCE?

FROM THE BEGINNINGS OF HISTORY MEN
have prayed to their gods. But have
the gods heard?

People have prayed morning, noon and
night. They have prayed alone in their
houses, in caves and on pillars; they have
prayed together in the market place, in
temples and on the mountain tops. They
have prayed in word, in dance, in painting,
as well as in the still, unbroken silence. They
have turned wheels, lit candles, poured out
libations and offered sacrifices. They have

stormed heaven's gates in order to gain the divine favor and protection. But have the gods heard?

There are false gods which are powerless, idols with eyes that see not and ears that near not. To pray to them is a superstitious waste of time. But God, we say, is no idol. He is the true God. He is a God who hears, he is God the Lord.

Yet what of the experience of Job, a good and godly man if ever there was one? 'I cry to thee and thou dost not answer me; I stand, and thou dost not heed me' (Job 30:20). What of the psalmist, echoing the thoughts of many before and after him? 'Why art thou so far from helping me, from the words of my groaning? O my God, I cry by day, but thou dost not answer, and by night, but find no rest' (Psalm 22:1-2).

Some Christians pray as if they have immediate access to God's will and utter certainty that their prayers will be answered. Others pray doggedly and determinedly, but without much life or hope. Prayer for them has become a formality and a duty. Others, again, have more or less given up the practice of prayer. It makes no difference. It is like a child crying in the night in an empty house. Nobody comes.

Prayer in some form or other is clearly of central importance in the Christian life. Without it Christian discipleship lapses into moral endeavor. But for many a Christian prayer remains a puzzling business, even something of an embarrassment. What do we really think we are doing when we make our prayers to God the Lord?

PRAYER AND MAGIC

Is prayer a kind of magic? Magic means power. The secret of magic is a hidden knowledge, a special technique. Master this technique and the world lies at your feet. What could be more appealing and more tempting to the weak, power-seeking, fantasy-building little child that lodges in the unconscious of many if not all of us?

We know, however, that prayer cannot be a form of magic. The practice of magic rests on the belief that things can be made to happen by the incantation of spells. Some words are thought to possess special powers, such that the forces of nature are subject to them. But the world of magic has gone for good. There is no room for it either in

science or in faith, however often we may
'touch wood' in order to avert ill-fortune.
Magic simply does not work. Furthermore,
we have been taught in Sunday School that
there is all the difference in the world
between prayer and magic. Prayer has to do
with God, whereas magic has nothing to do
with God. God cannot be compelled in the
way that magic seeks to compel.

Let us then bring God into the picture.
Now, of course, everthing changes. Or does
it?

PRAYER AND GETTING GOD
TO DO WHAT WE WANT

Certainly we shall no longer be thinking
of prayer as if it were something like an
automatic vending machine — put your
money in, press the right button and out
comes the item you want. God himself is
somehow or other involved in the process.
Perhaps prayer is more like an application to
a Higher Authority. There is nothing automatic about the outcome. It all depends on
the good will and cooperation of God himself and that, religiously speaking, is exactly
how it should be. Or is it? Has the spirit of

the whole operation in fact changed all that much?

Are we sure that we are not still thinking simply and solely in terms of getting what we want, only now by God's intervention rather than by magical incantation? Does God function like some kind of Celestial Official? You have to approach him because he holds the reins of power. Submit the proper application, singly or in triplicate, and there is at least an off-chance that your appeal will be successful. But is this really, religiously speaking, how things are?

Such behavior counts, I suppose, as prayer rather than magic. But what sort of God do we think we are praying to? What do we expect from him? What kind of relationship do we hope to have with him?

PRAYER FOR GOOD WEATHER

Not long ago a politician was photographed appealing for divine intervention in the prevailing weather conditions. 'Well', he is reported to have said, 'I've offered my prayers to the Almighty — we'll have to wait and see if there is a response.'

Was he being serious? Or was he having

a gentle joke at the Almighty's expense? Did he, or did anyone else, really believe that the Almighty would respond as requested? Once we start asking questions like this they almost tumble over each other. For example, might there have been more chance of a positive response if the prayers had been offered, not by a politician, but by, say, a minister of religion? Did anyone bother to wait in order to see whether in fact there was a positive response, if not immediate, miraculous, and undeniable, then in due course and in ways concealed from the public gaze? And when the weather did eventually improve, as improve it did, who was to say whether this was a natural and chance occurence or the result of a special act of divine providence?

What sort of God do we believe in? Does he modify the weather conditions in answer to prayer? Or does he reveal his universal care and concern for all by sending sunshine and rain on good and bad, deserving and undeserving alike? Or, as some would say, is such a universal care in reality the utter indifference of a 'God' who is no God at all?

Nor do questions arise only with regard

to the weather. What of prayers for victory in sport? What are we to make of tennis players who pray to God before playing that they may win, or of football players who go down on their knees to thank the Blessed Virgin Mary when they have scored a goal? Should not God, at least in some circumstances, simply let things take their course, prayer or no prayer? Would it not be grossly unfair if he were to intervene? For example, if I had done no work for my examination is it not attempted bribery to pray to God to help me pass and promise him my devotion if only he would do as I ask?

PRAYER AS A LAST RESORT

What sort of God do we believe in?

There is a story told in his diary by James Boswell of a sailor who had just returned from a sea voyage and who was asked what sort of trip he had had. 'Why', he replied, 'a very good one. We only had prayers twice, but one of the times there was no more occasion for them than if you and I should fall down and pray this minute.'

It is only too obvious what this sailor thought of God and prayer. They were for use in bad weather. Prayer was a kind of last resort emergency operation. When there was nothing left that could usefully be done to get out of trouble, then, and only then, was the time to turn to prayer. There was always the chance, even if only an outside chance, that it might do some good. In any case it could not do any harm. You could never be absolutely sure with God: he was too unpredictable.

THE UNPREDICTABILITY OF GOD

His unpredictability is one of the great problems that we have with God. There seems to be little or no clear pattern to his action. Sometimes he seems merciful and gracious, but all too often he seems silent and remote. So his unpredictability can assume alarming and threatening proportions. It comes to look like downright arbitrariness. And arbitrariness means carelessness. And carelessness means lovelessness. Someone suffering from cancer prays for a quick release — and recovers. Another suffering from the same illness prays for recovery — and dies. Does God play dice with human lives? If so, he is hardly a God whom we can love and worship. If he exists at all, he must be a monster.

What sort of God do we believe in? That remains the first and fundamental question.

USING GOD FOR OUR OWN ENDS

So long as we think of God in terms of unlimited power and of prayer as an attempt to get hold of some of that power for our own uses, to get God to do something for us, our outlook and attitude are not far removed from what they were when we were thinking of prayer in terms of pure magic. Our whole approach, in this case, is determined by the question whether prayer 'works', in the sense of producing the goods we want.

On this basis, if God does not appear to grant our requests, we wonder whether it is because we have failed to make them in the approved manner. Is God, perhaps, to be persuaded only if we go on asking, time and time again, as Jesus' own story of the importunate widow would at first seem to suggest (Luke 18:11)? The widow wanted justice againt her opponent. The judge could not be bothered and could not care less. But the

widow kept on pestering him until he granted
her suit in order to be done with her. She got
what she wanted by making a nuisance of
herself.

What are we to make of this story? Have
we to pressurize God in the way that the
widow pressurized the judge? Surely that
cannot be what Jesus meant!

Alternatively, we wonder whether there
are some kinds of requests that God is
willing to grant, others that he is unwilling.
Will he, for example, answer prayers for
health, but not for happiness; or for spiritual
goods, but not for material goods; or for
urgent and unusual needs, but not for the
ordinary and everyday requirements? Has he
a special list of his own approved charities?

What sort of God do we believe in?

So long as our minds run along crudely
utilitarian lines of getting God to do what we
want, most of us, I imagine, whether we are
believers or non-believers, would in our heart
of hearts admit that there generally seems to
be a better chance of getting something done
if we do it ourselves than if we ask God to
do it for us. It is not that we refuse to
believe the wonderful stories which some of
our fellow Christians tell of God's answers

to their prayers. It is rather that we cannot get out of our minds the thought of God's apparent failure to answer so many equally, if not more, deserving prayers. He may answer some people's prayers some of the time. But he cannot be relied on.

Piety suggests, perhaps, that we should not speak of God's failure to answer — God always answers — but of his answer 'No', of his refusal to grant this or that request. But then his 'Yes's' and his 'No's' are, as we remarked before, so unpredictable. If we are to judge simply by what people report, God's answers do not fall into any intelligible pattern. If we are to go on believing that, despite appearances, there is in fact an intelligible pattern because *God* must know best, then we have to be agnostic, that is, unknowing, about what God's purpose in any particular instance actually is. And such reluctant agnosticism can all too easily develop into a nagging suspicion that prayer is not, after all, a 'very good buy'.

The utilitarian approach to prayer, getting God to do what we want, is deeply entrenched in our minds because it appeals to that part of ourselves which prefers fantasy to reality. However, we simply must abandon this approach. It sets us off in the wrong direction. To ask if prayer 'works' is to think of it as a kind of magic, even if it is white magic. To put the point paradoxically, we shall never get a proper understanding of the 'use' of prayer until we have first considered its 'uselessness'.

THE 'VALIDITY' OF PRAYER

To speak of the 'uselessness' of prayer in this way is not to suggest that prayer is a waste of time and could well be given up. It is rather to remove prayer from among those activities of ours which have a 'use' over and above themselves and to place it among those which have a point and value of their own. We do not, for example, ask what is the use of playing tennis or of making music. These are not the kinds of activities which need to be justified by some further use and purpose which they serve beyond themselves. They are self-justifying. They have a value and validity of their own. They are, if you will grant the paradox, 'useless'.

So, too, with prayer. Prayer has a value and validity of its own. In *Little Gidding* T. S. Eliot speaks of the place 'where prayer has been valid'. Prayer is not a piece of spiritual technology. It is part and parcel of a living relationship. It is the inward aspect of our communion, or communication, with God. It is one way in which God is present to us and we are present to God.

We may, then, as a kind of shorthand, think of prayer in terms of presence rather than of power. There is a whole world of difference between, on the one hand, people trying to manipulate each other by the things they say to each other and, on the other hand, people sharing their thoughts with each other, their hopes and their fears, because they care for each other. In the first instance they are trying to use each other. In the second instance they have a regard for each other. So prayer can be either an attempt to manipulate God, or it can be a way of being with and sharing with God. Communication becomes an expression of communion.

In the chapters that follow we shall be trying to trace the main features of this communion between God and man and so to discover how prayer develops and deepens as the relationship between God and man develops and deepens. For the moment, however, we shall content ourselves with two very important observations.

PRAYER AS PERSONAL RELATIONSHIP

The first observation is this. Prayer is best understood on the analogy of a shared human relationship. The right context in which to understand prayer is the context of presence rather than power, after the pattern of a personal relationship rather than a market transaction.

Since this is the case, prayer must be something far richer and far deeper than a matter merely of making requests. Prayer is more than asking God to give us this or that.

Asking, as we shall see, need not and should not vanish away into thin air. Asking is the expression of desire, and the sharing of desire has its proper place even in the most sensitive and loving of human relationships. But it can no longer become the be-all and end-all of prayer. If there is no more to a human relationship than what each can get from the other, then the relationship is barely personal at all. Persons are being used, not appreciated and enjoyed.

Once, however, human beings are respected for what they are in themselves and regarded as ends rather than as means, then the relationships which are formed between persons acquire a value of their own, and as they develop they find expression in a rich variety of communication and communion.

At the center of such a relationship is an openness to each other. This makes possible and sustains a process of sharing, of giving and receiving. Persons share because they care, and in the process their whole selves are involved, together with all the varied resources of feeling, imagination and thought.

PRAYER AS PARTICIPATION

If the first point to be made is that prayer is best understood by comparing it with a shared human relationship, the second point to be made is that the analogy must not be pressed too far.

The relationship between man and God, though *like* a human relationship in so far as it is to be understood in personal rather than in impersonal terms, is in many significant ways *different* from a human relationship.

Human beings are finite creatures. Their

existence is bodily. They are located at a particular point in time and space. They are therefore external to one another, existing alongside and over against one another. They all possess their own private life and their own individual point of view. A large part of their interaction, therefore, depends on the giving and receiving of information, on learning to share another point of view.

God, on the other hand, is not a creature at all. He is Creator. Therefore he is not located in time and space and has no limited point of view. Rather than say that he has no point of view, since this suggests something abstract and impersonal, one might say that he embraces all points of view and makes them him own. He is always present with his creatures and with the eye of faith they can acknowledge his presence. But whether they acknowledge his presence or not, he is closer to them than they are to themselves.

There are a number of ways of trying to express God's presence in his creation. For example, we might say that God holds all his creatures in existence and that in him they live and move and have their being. We speak of him as omni-present and omni-

26

scient. If we speak and think of him as 'out there', we must not be misled by the language of space so as to imagine that he is alongside his world, as human beings are alongside each other. Rather we are drawing attention to the fact that he is other than the world, that he 'transcends' it. If we speak and think of him as 'within', we must not confine him to some inner world of human consciousness, but rather draw attention to the fact that he is at the heart and center of all that exists, 'immanent' in the world he creates. Just how God can be completely other than the world and at the same time fully present in the world is a mystery. Perhaps we can shed some light on the mystery if we think of our own human experience. Sometimes we seem able to express ourselves fully in what we say and do, yet at other times we feel that nothing can express our deepest selves.

Since God is Creator rather than creature, our relationship with him in prayer cannot take the form of an ordinary dialogue between two human beings. He does not have to be brought into a conversation. His attention does not have to be gained. We do not have to inform him of what is going on in our minds. We do not have to put our thoughts into words in order that we may be heard. We do not have to listen for a heavenly voice as the partner in our conversation. Our conversation with God need not take the form of a dialogue at all — though that is not to suggest that it is really only a monologue. To use the first definition of the word which is to be found in the Shorter Oxford Dictionary, our 'conversation' with God is 'the action of living and having one's being' with God. Talking is not the only form of 'being with.'

The essence of communication is sharing, or participation. For Christians this sharing with God has been described as 'the fellowship of the Holy Spirit', or, as the New English Bible has it, 'fellowship in the Holy Spirit' (2 Cor. 13:14).

What sort of fellowship, sharing, communication is this?

What sort of God do we really believe in?

II.
IN THE SPIRIT

FATHER, SON, HOLY SPIRIT

BEFORE WE CAN GET MUCH FURTHER
with our question whether God
answers prayer, we must, as we have
already seen, link this question with another,
namely, what sort of God it is that we believe in. What is he like?

We might start by drawing up a list of his
characteristics. For example, he is, we might
say, holy and mighty, or wise and just, or
loving and merciful. Or, better still, we
might say that he is all these things, and

others, together. He is all-powerful, all-knowing, all-good. He is certainly not a god to be used, or cajoled, or bullied.

We might also say that the specially Christian idea of God is a trinitarian idea. God is Father, Son, Holy Spirit, three in one and one in three.

Such language may seem to some to be nothing but a piece of theological jargon, making what is, at least in theory, a simple and straightforward matter into an unnecessarily complicated business.

The doctrine of the Trinity has always been something of a stumbling block to the ordinary believer. Or if it has not exactly been a stumbling block, then it has at any rate been something to be accepted on trust but without comprehension. Why then introduce it into the simple pieties of prayer? Surely it is good enough to pray simply to 'God' and to leave it at that?

Sometimes, however, theology itself stems from the experience of prayer. So it ought to be able to assist us in understanding prayer. In fact trinitarian language is of special value when it comes to prayer. It is a kind of shorthand, a useful reminder, which can help us, when we begin to pray, to start off on the right foot and not get bogged down in an attempt to have a conversation with a partner who has the disconcerting habit of never appearing and never uttering a word.

In the rich, many-sided, classical Christian tradition it has been widely taught that, when Christians pray to God, they should offer their prayers in the name of the Father and of the Son and of the Holy Spirit. To be still more precise, they should pray *to* the Father, *through* the Son, and *in* the Holy Spirit.

What does this mean?

GOD AS FATHER

God is and remains in many respects the great Unknown, the ultimate Mystery. We need some way of thinking about him which, while doubtless in the end inadequate, at least sets our hearts and minds moving in the right direction. We need, that is, a reminder that the God whom we are approaching is the Ultimate Mysterious Being of all that is, the Creator of all things visible and invisible, not some petty and perverse idol which we have constructed in our own image. When we approach God in prayer, we have a lot to unlearn as well as a lot to learn.

At the same time we also need to be reassured that this mysterious God welcomes our approach to him and hears our prayers, that as we draw near to the fire of his presence we shall be purified and enlightened, not burnt to ashes.

When, then, we pray *to the Father,* we are acknowledging both God's holiness and his loving-kindness.

We are launching out into the deep, reaching forward into the mysterious and unknown, throwing our prayers up into the air in the hope that they may find a hold and become a ladder between earth and heaven. 'Father' reminds us that the God whom we approach is Alpha and Omega, the beginning and the end, the origin and goal of all that exists, the hidden God whose felt absence is as real and compelling an experience as is His felt presence. No wonder some find it fitting and appropriate to kneel in order to pray!

But 'Father' means much more than that. If our experience of God were only one of awe and amazement before the majesty of over-arching Mystery, we might well feel wonder and even humility in his presence,

but we should hardly have cause to approach
him in trust, hope and love. Yet trust, hope
and love - or faith, hope and charity - are
precisely those characteristics which are
appropriate to man's relationship with God,
as Christians are invited to understand it.
Hence we may come to God our Father with
'full confidence', the Greek word for which
is used in this connection by more than one
New Testament writer, for it occurs in the
letters of Paul and of John, as well as in the
Letter to the Hebrews (cf. Eph. 3:12; 1 Tim.
3:13; 1 John 3:21; 5 14; Hebrews 4:16;
10:35).

On what is this confidence based?
Certainly not on our own merits or achievements. Left to ourselves we should be more
likely to keep out of God's way, to hide
from his presence when, as the Genesis story
delightfully puts it, we hear 'the sound of the
Lord God walking in the garden in the cool
of the day' (Genesis 3:8). Reality is often
more than we can bear, the reality about
ourselves as well as the reality of the world
in which we live. And what is God if not the
God of reality and truth?

When we speak of God's holiness, we
often find it difficult to give the idea much

content, except that we have a feeling that there is a vast distance between ourselves and God, and that he keeps himself to himself. There is an element of truth in this feeling. There is indeed a vast distance between man and God, between creature and Creator. Furthermore, God cannot be other than he is, and whatever else he is, he is the pure light of truth. Fantasy, make-believe, pretense often have a greater attraction for us men and women than the truth, but with God there can be no falsehood or deceit. In the words of the Fourth Gospel, 'Here lies the test: the light has come into the world, but men preferred darkness to light because their deeds were evil' (John 3:19 NEB). The Greek word for 'test' also means 'judgment' and 'separation'. Thus it is not the self-sufficiency and stand-offishness of God that keeps him at a distance. It is our human sin that drives us asunder.

GOD AS SON

If the confidence that we have in the presence of God does not derive from our own merits or achievements, it must come from outside of us. We have to receive it as a gift. It is in fact, Christians affirm, a gift of God himself, effected and made real for man *through* Jesus Christ.

This theme of God's gift of confidence through Jesus Christ, and of his gracious invitation to man to draw near to him, is developed in the third chapter of the Letter to the Ephesians and summarized in verses eleven and twelve. 'This is in accord with his (i.e. God's) age-long purpose, which he achieved in Christ Jesus our Lord. In him we have access to God with freedom, in the confidence born of trust in him.'

Thus it is because we have faith in the person and work of Jesus Christ, and in the new relationship with God which he has established for us, that we now have the courage and confidence to address God as 'Father'. He is the 'Father', and we can pray to him with the same freedom and confidence as when a child speaks with his own familiar father.

In praying to God, then, we pray '*to* the Father *through* the Son'. We approach him as 'our Father', because we know him as 'Father of Jesus Christ'. But what is meant by praying also '*in* the Spirit'?

GOD AS SPIRIT

Some people have an idea that prayer 'in the Spirit' is a kind of trance or intoxication. They imagine that, when the 'Spirit' takes hold of a person, he loses his self-control, and words comes to his lips unbidden and from God knows where, some of them perhaps intelligible, but most of them unintelligible. Is such an idea necessarily right?

In much of biblical thought 'spirit' represents a force like the wind. It can appear out of the blue, take hold of a man beyond his control and make him speak or act in a way which would ordinarily be quite impossible. Spirit can overwhelm a man's normally rational behavior and produce ecstatic phenomena, or it can deepen and enhance his rational powers of insight and judgment. Furthermore, spirit can be of God or of the devil. Hence care and discrimination are necessary.

For Paul the Spirit of God is one with the Spirit of Jesus Christ. The same God who was present to Jesus from his birth to his death is now present through the risen Christ to his people the Church. Hence the believer's relationship to God is no formal or external one. It is a living relationship of heart and mind. It gives him a new life and liberty in the community of fellow-believers. It is the Spirit which unites believers in the 'body' of Christ.

Can we translate this language of 'spirit' into a more modern idiom? If so, we might do something to bridge the gap which yawns between the language of 'spirit' and 'spirituality', which belongs almost exclusively to a religious ghetto, and the language which we use to speak of ordinary human existence and activity.

SPIRIT AND FREEDOM

Everything that exists in the world is, we are told, made up of the same basic units of energy. These units interact with each other, and in this process different patterns, or systems, are formed and maintained. We human beings, as much as anything else, are systems of energy. We act upon our environment and our environment acts upon us. We are part of nature, a complex part, undoubtedly, but still a part. Thus many of our reactions are predictable, rather like those of a machine. If we are hungry, we look for food; if we are tired, we fall asleep; if we are attacked, either we fight back or we run away.

Not all our actions, however, are easily predictable in this way. Because we are human beings, and not machines, our responses cannot always be reduced to those of even the most complicated machines. Our senses, feelings, imagination, thoughts, values and decisions may all be involved in the responses we make to our environment. We discover ourselves selecting, interpreting, evaluating. The more we do so, the more we make our responses our very own. We become responsive. We accept responsibility. We become, in a measure, 'free' men and women.

As human beings, then, we are part of nature, but we can rise above nature. We are what we are because the past has made us what we are, but we need not necessarily be slaves to the past. By understanding how we have become what we are, we have taken the first step towards freeing ourselves from slavery to the past. We can now have a say in what we shall be in the future. The past is closed, but the future is to some extent open.

It is this capacity for responsiveness and

responsibility, for openness and freedom, which has traditionally been called 'spirit'. Sometimes it has been said that human beings live in two worlds, the world of nature and the world of spirit. But the drawback to this way of talking is that it breaks up the unity of the one world we know. In so doing it does less than justice to the 'natural', while banishing the 'spiritual' to the 'supernatural' and the 'extraordinary'.

When we speak of God as 'Spirit', we are, then, speaking of him as the One who is totally free, totally responsive, and totally responsible. He is the One who can make the old new and give life to the dead. He it is who calls us to be free, responsive and responsible.

Thus it is 'in the Spirit' that we open ourselves to this God, who is the source and center of all energy and activity, including our own. It is 'in the Spirit' that we may dare to lose ourselves in the hope of finding ourselves. For 'the Spirit' is life, liberty, love. If in trust and love we open ourselves to God our Father in the Spirit of Jesus Christ, we may confidently expect to become more 'ourselves', more free, more alive, not by our own unaided efforts, but by what

God himself gives to us. We live; yet it is not we who live, but Christ who lives in us (cf. Gal. 2:20).

This attempt to translate the traditional imagery of spirit-possession into a more modern idiom may, like all translations, have been more confusing than helpful! But its main purpose will have been achieved if it has suggested that prayer 'in the Spirit' has nothing necessarily to do with extraordinary, ecstatic or paranormal phenomena. Rather it is prayer which touches the living center of a person's being — both the conscious and the unconscious combined — and links that center with the creative center of all being in a rhythm of receiving and responding. When we pray we participate in God's own being, we share in his action and respond to his love. For in God being and action and love are eternally one.

The way in which Christian prayer finds its own special pattern and power is clearly set forth in a collect such as the following:

> O God our Father, giver of light and life,
> send thy holy Spirit into our hearts;
> and grant us thoughts better than our
>   own thoughts,

prayers deeper than our own prayers,
and powers beyond our own powers;
that we may walk in the ways of truth
    and love,
through Jesus Christ our Lord.

Such a collect has a threefold pattern. It is prayer 'to' our Father. It is offered 'through' his Son. And it acclaims the presence of God's spirit 'in' our hearts. At the same time it is a single activity. It seeks and expects the interpenetration of the human by the divine.

To sum up. When we pray 'in the Spirit', or when we preface our prayers with the invocation 'in the name of the Father and of the Son and of the Holy Spirit', we are giving a certain shape to our praying and we are embodying certain convictions about its nature and significance.

Let us now set out what some of these fundamental convictions are.

PRAYER AS PART OF A
FULLER RELATIONSHIP

First, prayer is part and parcel of a living and growing relationship with God that extends into every corner of life.

In so far as we are focusing our lives on the center of all being, living towards God, acknowledging his presence, seeking his will and responding to his love, we are living prayerfully. Prayer can be an attitude as well as an act. Just as someone's behavior can be thoughtful, even when he is not self-consciously thinking, so a person's life can be prayerful, even when he is not self-consciously saying his prayers. If this were not so, Paul's injunction to 'pray without ceasing' (1 Thess. 5:17) would be utter nonsense!

When we speak of someone living prayerfully we mean that prayer colors the whole of that person's life. It is not an awkward and disconnected part. Important as specific acts of prayer undoubtedly are — no one can be thoughtful if he never sits back and thinks! — they have their place and purpose within a fuller and continuing relationship. Speaking with God is one way of being with God.

GOD AT THE CENTER

Second, since prayer is part and parcel of

a living relationship with God, and not just a device for getting him to do what we want, it draws our attention away from ourselves and towards God.

God is at the center of our prayers as much as he is at the center of our lives. Prayer begins with him, not simply in the sense that his name and his Kingdom and his will become the first and foremost matters of our concern, as Jesus made clear in the prayer which he taught his own disciples, but also in the sense that the whole relationship has its beginning and its continuing with God himself. We do not have to get the business of prayer under way. God is already at prayer, reaching out to us, calling us, moving within our hearts. For us to pray is to be drawn into his prayer, just as for us to live is to be drawn into his life.

If God often appears to be distant and unapproachable, as indeed he does, it is because we are remote from him, not because he is remote from us. In Jesus' parable of the shepherd and his search, it was the sheep that was lost, not the shepherd. God draws near to us long before we draw near to him.

There is, of course, a long history of

man's search for God. But there is a longer history of God's search for man. The coming of Jesus is the expression in the person and life of a single human being of God's eternal coming to his world. Man's spiritual longing for God is itself a response to God's spiritual longing for man.

So Paul writes that 'the Spirit comes to the aid of our weakness. We do not even know how we ought to pray, but through our inarticulate groans the Spirit himself is pleading for us, and God who searches our inmost being knows what the Spirit means, because he pleads for God's own people in God's own way' (Romans 8:26-7).

In another striking image the author of the Letter to the Hebrews speaks of the perpetual priesthood of Jesus, mediating between man and God: 'That is why he is also able to save absolutely those who approach God through him; he is always living to plead on their behalf' (Hebrews 7:25).

The basis for all our prayer is in God himself. He is the source and fount of all life and love, because he is himself life and love, and what he is himself flows forth into the whole of his creation. So he is always seeking to win from his human creatures their own free response of love. This means that our prayer to God is always his gift to us before it can become our own attainment. We must receive before we can offer.

GOD'S GIFT OF HIMSELF

Third, what God has to offer us in our relationship with him is above all else himself. That is his supreme gift. Whatever he may or may not be said to 'do' in 'answer' to our prayer, it is the prayer of communion which he himself is ever seeking to initiate and to sustain. Whatever may or may not come to pass in the course of events as a result of prayer, God draws us towards himself and, in so doing, shares with us his own life. What greater gift could he give?

Jesus taught his disciples: 'Set your mind on the kingdom of God and his justice before anything else, and the rest will come to pass as well' (cf. Matt. 6:33). We might paraphrase his teaching as follows: put God at the center of your thoughts and desires, the center which is rightfully his, and everything else will find its own proper place.

There is a sense in which it is profoundly true to say that when God gives himself he has nothing more to give. 'All things are yours: present or future, life or death, all is yours; and you are Christ's; and Christ is God's' (cf. 1 Cor. 3:21-3).

In prayer we acknowledge and celebrate God's life in and for the world, and in prayer we offer our life in the world to his glory. Life in all its different aspects becomes an engagement with the divine Love, and prayer becomes the language of that engagement.

PRAYER AND COMMUNITY

Fourth, our relationship with God, personal through and through, is nevertheless not something private and apart. It is to be lived out in community and in the world. It is a sharing with God and it is also a sharing with our neighbor.

Since God is Creator as well as Redeemer, his care and concern extend into every aspect of the life of the world, which is the object of his love. Thus the deepening of our relationship with him does not draw us away from the world, but sends us out into the world.

Some people think that life in the world
is hard to reconcile with a life lived for God,
and that therefore we should try to shut out
the world when we pray. But this is true only
when the world threatens to take the place of
God. It is perhaps a pity that the writer of
the Fourth Gospel so often uses the single
word 'world' to describe creation when it
sets itself up against God and goes its own
way in forgetfulness of him. This 'world' is
indeed God-forsaken, but not because God
has forsaken it, rather because it has forsak-
en God. Jesus' disciples clearly do not belong to this 'world'. But their lives are to be
lived out in the world, which is God's
appointed place for them, and not in some
other-worldly kingdom. The center of their
lives is to be God, not themselves or anything other than God. But the circle of which
God is the center is the whole created order,
the world which is the object of his love.

In the context of God's care and concern
for the whole of his creation prayer becomes
the inward shaping of a relationship between
God and man which is to be expressed in the
ordinary world of everyday life.

Prayer discovers the presence of the divine within the ordinary. It is part of the

whole process of turning to God, of seeing all things in God, and of being transformed according to the likeness of God. It is a kind of transfiguration. Prayer makes a difference. Paul expresses this idea in writing to the Christians at Rome: 'I implore you by God's mercy to offer your very selves to him: a living sacrifice, dedicated and fit for his acceptance, the worship offered by mind and heart. Adapt yourselves no longer to the pattern of this present world, but let your minds be remade and your whole nature thus transformed. Then you will be able to discern the will of God, and to know what is good, acceptable, and perfect' (Rom. 12:1, 2).

If, in the light of what we have been saying about the relationship between God and man in the world, we now turn back to the original question, 'Does prayer work?', we find that it is beginning to take on a very different significance from that which at first it seemed to possess. No longer is it a frankly utilitarian question, 'Does prayer produce the goods?'. Rather it is more like the question, 'Is prayer an essential part of the good life?'. In other words, is a right relationship between man and God in the world nourished and developed through fellowship in the Spirit? Is prayer a life-giving reality and not a piece of self-deluding make-believe?

Before, however, we say more about prayer in terms of presence and relationship, let us have another look at some of the tangles which we get into when we forget that the God who is Father of Jesus Christ always wills to give his creatures what is for their good and that the greatest good that he can give them is the gift of himself.

III.
WHY DOESN'T GOD . . . ?

WE MAY SAY THAT GOD KNOWS best, but with the best will in the world we find it hard to believe that it is really so. If we are honest with ourselves we have to admit that, were we in charge of everything, we should have arranged it all very differently!

UNANSWERED PRAYER

Why, for example, does God not do more for those who cry out to him in their distress? He encourages them to turn to him. He promises them a land flowing with milk and honey. But when it comes to the crunch he just does not seem to be around. And this makes prayer such a chancy and frustrating business.

Suppose, for instance, that someone is seriously ill. He has been brought up as a Christian and knows that an important part of Jesus' ministry was to heal the sick. So he prays to God to restore him to health. He gets others to pray for him as well, his family, his friends and members of his local church. There is a vast cloud of prayer rising up to heaven on his behalf.

If he recovers, we say that God has heard our prayers and we thank him for his grace and goodness. If his recovery goes against all medical expectations, we say that God still works miracles.

Suppose, however, that he does not recover. Suppose that he dies. What about God's goodness then? We begin to be confused. If God can work miracles, why did he not work a miracle here and now? Why does he work his miracles so seldom? Is he tight-fisted with his generosity?

We feel a little guilty. If it is not God

who is to blame — and you really are not supposed to go around blaming God, despite the fact that the psalmist on occasion seems to have done just that! — then we must be the ones who are to blame.

What went wrong? Was there something amiss with our prayers? And with ourselves too?

PRAYING HARDER

Perhaps we should have prayed harder.

But what does 'praying harder' actually mean? Should we have prayed more often? Should our prayers have been longer, more fervent, more single-minded, more compelling? Should we perhaps have got even more people together to pray for the sick person? Are the prayers of many people more effective than the prayers of only a few? Do numbers count with God?

We can feel that there is something really rather silly about these questions, but we may find it difficult to put our finger on where exactly the silliness lies.

Not far below the surface of these questions lies the thought that God, like some enormous snowball, has to be pushed into activity. Our prayers then become a moving force. The greater the force, the more likely is God to be moved.

We know that this is really all nonsense, and that our relationship with God cannot be like that at all. But the idea is difficult to get rid of. It is all too easy to think and talk of the power and effectiveness of prayer. What is needed, from this point of view, is more powerful prayer. If only we could turn up the spiritual voltage, as it were, and so make God jump to it. In terms of the power of prayer the organization of prayer groups comes to resemble the mounting of a military operation!

Once uncertainty, anxiety and a sense of guilt have got a hold, they are not easily dispersed. We wonder whether our prayers failed, not because there was something wrong with the prayers themselves, but because there was something wrong with us.

NOT ENOUGH FAITH?

Could it have been that we did not have enough faith? Was there a fatal germ of doubt in our praying right from the word go? 'Whatever you ask in prayer', Jesus himself is reported to have said, 'believe that you receive it, and you will' (Mark 11:24). Did we fail our friend because of our lack of belief?

It is not always easy to know for certain what exactly Jesus said and meant, because no one was taking down his words as he spoke them, and we do not always know the situations in which he spoke them. But the words which we quoted in the last paragraph cannot be taken just as they stand. Surely it cannot be true to say without qualification that we shall get what we pray for if only we believe that our prayers are being answered. There must, then, be some deliberate exaggeration. 'It is not true to say prayers are answered because we believe that we have received our request' (see V. Taylor, *The Gospel according to St. Mark* [Macmillan 1959], p. 467). But what can the point of the exaggeration be? Very likely these words are intended to emphasize the importance of truthfulness and trust in prayer. There must be no pretense. Integrity matters. Prayer must be rooted in what we really are and really believe and really want. It is no use our pretending with God. Prayer involves our real selves, mixed up as they are, or it is nothing. And our real selves, when offered to God, can become instruments of his purposes.

Prayer is meant to be a deep engagement with God, just as it was for Jacob, who wrestled all night with the 'angel of the Lord' and refused to let him go until he had given him a blessing (see Genesis 32). Prayer such as this can 'move mountains' (cf. Jesus' other imaginative exaggeration recorded in the same context, Mark 11:22-3).

It would be a mistake to suppose, on the basis of a literal interpretation of Jesus' words, that, if some particular longed-for and prayed-for event fails to come to pass, this is because we have been doubting with part of ourselves whether in fact it will come to pass. Believing that something will be the case does not make it the case. Whatever belief and faith may be, they are not that kind of nonsensical hocus-pocus. Wanting, hoping, asking, trusting, all enter into a deep engagement with God. But faith is not wishful thinking and prayer is not a means of wish-fulfillment. Our communion with God is not to be reduced to that level of transaction.

God knows our innermost thoughts. He

knows that we are a mixture of trust and hope on the one hand and of fear and doubt on the other. It is not our openly acknowledged fears and doubts which keep us from his presence. The centurion's confession of faith, 'Lord, I believe: help my unbelief' (Mark 9:24), can be our confession of faith. It has the ring of truthfulness. What hinders our prayers is our hypocrisy, when we acknowledge before God only that part of ourselves which we fondly believe will please and persuade him, so making of the living God a dumb idol and of prayer a superstitious pretense.

DOES GOD REFUSE TO HEAR SINNERS?

Not only our doubts can make us feel guilty. Our sins and failures can make us feel guilty too. If it is the case that 'the prayer of a righteous man has great power in its effects' (James 5:16 NEB), we wonder whether the apparent ineffectiveness of our own prayers is due to our unrighteousness. Perhaps we are just not good enough to have our prayers answered. Did we fail our friend because of the sinfulness of our lives?

Once again we are being tempted to turn

our prayer into a kind of work. What we are implying in fastening upon our feelings of guilt is that we might in theory be good enough to deserve to have our prayers heard.

Once stated, the absurdity of this idea is obvious. We know that our relationship with God cannot be based on merit. If we got what we deserved, we should all be in deep trouble.

God is love, and love does not wait to be deserved. It reaches out of its own accord. Hence our communion with God is based on the graciousness of the divine love, not on the merits of human righteousness. It is love that kindles prayer and keeps it alight, God's prior love for us and our responsive love for him. This is not to say that goodness and righteousness are not important in the Christian life. That would be absurd. But they are not the basis either of faith or of prayer. The basis is love. Both creation and redemption are the expression of divine love. Thus it is through Jesus Christ and in the power of his Spirit, not through ourselves and in the power of our own achievements, that we have the confidence that our Father welcomes and hears our prayers.

No matter how hard we try, we find that

we cannot altogether get rid of our feelings of guilt. However, as we look around for excuses, we may hit upon the following way of pushing these feelings to one side.

RESIGNATION TO THE WILL OF GOD

The thought occurs to us that what has in fact come to pass, despite our prayers to the contrary, must have been meant to come to pass. After all, God, we are taught, knows what is for the best and has everything under control. From our limited point of view what has occurred may look like a senseless tragedy, but we see only a small part of the total picture, whereas God sees the whole picture. Perhaps even the dark parts of the picture contribute to the effect of the picture as a whole. Anyhow, it is not for us to question God's will, but to accept it. 'Whatever will be, will be.'

Such piety sounds very Christian. After all, Christians are supposed to accept God's will, even if they do not understand it. And God's ways are not as our ways.

There is some truth in this. We do have to walk by faith and not by sight. There are times when it looks and feels as if God has abandoned us, an experience such as Jesus himself is said to have undergone: 'My God, my God, why hast thou forsaken me?' (Mark 15:34). In such times faith needs to call upon courage, perseverance, and hope.

All the same, there is something dangerously amiss with the thinking which goes with 'accepting God's will' in this way. Are we really to believe that whatever happens is according to God's will?

It sounds very humble to answer that we should believe just this. Are we not confessing our belief that God is almighty and omnipotent? Are we not acknowledging his power, besides which there is no other power? And when things happen, as happen they do, which do not look like the handiwork of God, is it not simply our ignorance which justifies us in asserting that they must be part of the one divine plan?

God the Ruler, God the All-Powerful, God the Supreme Disposer. All these images and pictures of what God is like emphasize his power to create and to destroy, to decree what shall be and what shall not be, to plan and control the course of nature and history. They harmonize well with a notion of prayer as an attempt to tap the ultimate source of power. But they are fatally one-sided, a kind of distorting mirror of the truth. If we accept them as the whole truth and nothing but the truth, they are at best misleading, at worst demonic.

Taken at face value these images of God make him directly responsible for all the evils that happen in the world. And that turns God into a monster, something like Thomas Hardy's 'President of the Immortals'. Hardy's grim story of Tess of the d'Urbervilles ends with Tess' execution. Hardy comments:' "Justice" was done, and the President of the Immortals . . . had ended his sport with Tess.'

But God, puzzling, mysterious, awesome as he is, does not sport with his creatures. God, Christians believe, is like Jesus Christ. Jesus never 'sported' with sinners. He never used the powers he possessed in order to dominate. 'The Son of man came not to be served but to serve' (Mark 10:45). His power was the 'power' of love. To be like God was to give, not to manipulate.

If God is like Jesus Christ, if he is 'Father' of Jesus Christ, then his power, too, is the power of love. His love is pure and unbounded. When we think of his power, we must think of it in terms of such love. Love like this cannot by any stretch of the imagination be held directly responsible for everything that occurs in the world. It is all very well to talk in terms of the goodness of the picture as a whole, and to suggest that this justifies the badness of this or that part of the picture. But it is not at all well if you yourself happen to be the poor wretch who endures and suffers just that part. If God is love, he cares for the parts as well as for the whole.

A submissive and seemingly pious resignation contains the seeds of a callous and impious blasphemy.

Jesus himself prayed, 'Thy kingdom come, thy will be done, on earth as in heaven'. Obviously God's will was not being done, his rule was not yet fully operative. Life was more like a battle-ground between good and evil, light and darkness, and this battle-ground extended far beyond the sphere of human actions. There is no need to take language about Satan and demons with a wooden literalness. But it does point to the fact that there are in the world forces of destruction as well as forces of creativity, processes of breaking down as well as of building up.

Does this mean that God has abdicated his position as Creator and Redeemer and that the world is now out of his control? Is our trust in God misplaced?

Not at all. God was, is and always will be the source and ground of all created things. Even Satan and his angels, to use the biblical imagery, are only created things. The power they exercise is not, as such, an ultimate threat to God. It has its limits, as does all created power. The question remains: why does it exist at all? Why does God allow so much evil in his world?

It would be idle to pretend that there is an easy, indisputable answer to this question. But perhaps we can detect the beginnings of an answer, sufficient to enable faith to live with the question rather than to be destroyed by it.

DIVINE POWER AND DIVINE LOVE

We must rethink our ideas of God's power in accordance with the way in which that power was expressed in the life of Jesus. It must be all of a piece. We must think of the divine power, as we have already suggested, in terms of the power of love. But what does that imply?

Love is a slippery elastic notion. It can mean many different things. It is very easily sentimentalized. We need to learn the true meaning of divine love and to be taught its heights and depths, its severity as well as its gentleness, its righteousness as well as its pity. It is, as the author of the Letter to the Hebrews says, 'a fearful thing to fall into the hands of the living God' (Hebrews 10:31). But this is not because God sports with us as if we were his playthings, or weighs our good actions against our bad actions like some blind Justice. It is because his love pursues us and will not finally forsake us.

LOVE, FREEDOM AND RISK

Love requires freedom. It makes nonsense to think that love can compel or manipulate a loving response. In giving freedom love has to let go. So parents have to learn to let their children go, to withdraw their direct control, to give them space in which to be themselves. So lovers have to respect each other's 'otherness'. If the one dominates and controls the other, there can be no growth of love, only the violence of manipulation. But letting go, respecting otherness, does not involve ceasing to care. Love continues to desire and to seek the good of the beloved. It longs and works for the wonder of a renewed and deeper relationship.

So God's relationship with his creation is a relationship in which he wills it to be free in order that his human creatures may be free. Because he is love he withdraws a space from the world in order to let it be itself. He lets it go in order to let it be. He gives it a real measure of independence. But he does not cease to care for his world. And he does not cease to work in and for his world. He comes. He calls. He shares. He gives and forgives. He creates and recreates.

In the Fourth Gospel there is a repeated emphasis on the coming and going of Jesus from and to his Father (see, for example, chapters 13-17). If we take it literally this language is very puzzling. If, however, we take it symbolically to express the inner movement of love, of being and letting be, of letting go and winning back, of withdrawal and return, of making a space and building a bridge, it represents the kind of relationship which God has with his creation.

Love, we may say, creates in freedom and for freedom. So when God creates his world, he creates it by 'persuading' it to create itself.

Love's creation necessarily involves experiment and risk. Freedom without risk is no freedom at all. The creation of divine Love is a venture. There will be casualties as well as triumphs. But Love will never forsake even the casualties.

When the psalmist speaks of creation, he speaks of the divine word of command. 'He spake the word, and they were made; he commanded, and they were created' (Psalm 148:5). Such language emphasizes the fact that the whole world of nature in its variety of manifestations, all things visible and invisible, are not there just by chance. They are to be traced back to the creative will and purposes of God. Without him they would have no being at all. Nevertheless this language of the divine command can mislead. Love commends more often than it commands. Love by its very nature imposes limits on the arbitrariness of sheer power. Love needs both space and time in which to bring forth its creative work. Love as Creator cannot create without seeking and awaiting the creature's own response.

There are, then, many things which sheer power can do but which boundless love cannot do. When we cry out, in some moment of agonized distress, 'Why doesn't God do something about it?', our cry suggests that God *could* do something about it *if only he would.* We assume that God, as God, has the power to do anything that he will. 'Why doesn't he?' comes to mean 'Why won't he?'. Why does God remain unmoved by his children's cries?

In a sense, no doubt, God is free to do as he wills. There is nothing outside of himself that can compel him to do what he does not will. However, because he is Love there are many things that he cannot will. Love, even boundless love, is in its very nature self-limiting.

Since God is Love, he cannot be distant, unmoved, inactive. He does not have to be implored to come near. The love of human being waxes and wanes, but God's love is unquenchable.

If we take this truth to heart, then we can be sure that *God is already doing all that Love can do.*

If, when we pray to him, God does not

intervene in the way we want and expect, it is because, being the sort of God he is, he cannot intervene. Boundless love does not possess unbounded power. 'If thou be the Christ, save yourself and us', says the impatient thief. But Jesus, just because he is the Christ, cannot. And God cannot. Love's path to life may be the way of the cross.

Our trust in God is not grounded in his power to do absolutely anything. God is not omnipotent, in that sense of the word. Our trust, rather, is grounded in his inexhaustible love, which we believe to be mighty in and through all things. 'I am sure that neither death, nor life, nor angels, nor principalities, nor things present, nor things to come, nor powers, nor height, nor depth, nor anything else in all creation, will be able to separate us from the love of God in Christ Jesus our Lord' (Romans 8:38-9).

Trust in God's inexhaustible love can be sorely tested by the way things go in the world. If we abandon the comforting idea of divine omnipotence, we shall find faith more of a venture, less of a certainty. Even when we take full note of Love's inherent self-limitation, there is much that we find almost impossible to understand. Yet we have the assurance that God is with us, even in those times when he seems absent from us. And love engenders both faith and hope.

So much for fundamentals. But can we say more about God's way, Love's way, with the world?

IV.
GOD'S WAY WITH THE WORLD

W E HAVE ARGUED THAT THE GOD whom we have learned to call the Father of Jesus Christ, and whose attitudes and activities are all of a piece with those of his Son, cannot be an omnipotent Ruler who directly manipulates everything that happens in the world as if it were a puppet-show. God is Love. And divine Love, as we have seen, expresses himself by letting go and letting be, making room for his creation to be itself and to do its own thing.

We should expect to find, then, in the

world around us something like what we do in fact find, separate but interdependent bundles of energy, all interacting in a mixture of conflict and cooperation, order and disorder, good and ill, chance and necessity. In many respects it has a very human aspect and resembles the relationships we find within an ordinary human family!

AN OBSERVER GOD?

But does this mean that God has completely excluded himself from all that goes on in the world? Is he more like a benevolent but long-lost Uncle than a loving Father? Does the world go its own way as if there were no God at all? And must our prayer take account of his non-intervention?

There is, perhaps, a good deal to be said in favor of a view such as this. For example, we should have a clear and compelling answer to all our questions beginning, 'Why doesn't God . . . ?' God does not do this or do that, because God does not 'do' anything. In his benevolence he leaves everyone and everything well alone. He does not interfere. He brought the world into being in the first place, but once it had begun its evolutionary course he let it develop in its own way. He does not act in it either by providence or by miracle. He watches over it but has no further say in it. He is an observer but not a participant.

This view, moreover, fits rather well with our scientific view of the world.

The more we understand the way things go in the world, the more we are convinced that they proceed according to their own intrinsic principles. Physics, chemistry, biology and all the other sciences explain things in terms of impersonal structures and chance occurrences. Things are what they are now because they are the natural and predictable outcome of what they were a moment ago. Furthermore, God does not create by some special act each new stage in the evolutionary process. Each stage develops by random change and environmental adaptation from the preceding stage.

This view of God's relationship to the world is attractive to many people who wish to retain their belief in God but who believe that the scientific understanding of the world, which they also wish to adopt, rules out all idea of God's activity in the world.

THE GOD OF THE DEISTS

A very similar view was put forward in the seventeenth and eighteenth centuries by thinkers who were known as Deists. Deism is the view that the world was created by a good and wise Supreme Being, who planned it, brought it into being but after that did not intervene in its working. The scientific theory inherent in Deism was that the world was rather like a perfectly constructed machine. Once it had been made, it kept on going without further ado. The associated religious theory was that God was an intelligent and benevolent Designer, who destined righteous souls for immortality. The orderliness of the world proved that it had been made by God, and man's sense of duty told him what was God's will.

There was no need of any special revelation to make God known. Indeed all appeal to alleged revelations, as to any other alleged miracles, was sheer superstition. Religious knowledge was simply a rational extension of scientific knowledge.

For the Deist, prayer was the sort of humble address that a rational creature would make to this Supreme Rational Being.

It would express the appropriate acknowledgment and praise, but not much else. To say that such prayer, judged by more traditional criteria, was stilted and restrained is no doubt true. To say that it was cold and lacked all religious feeling and sensitivity would be to misrepresent it. Joseph Addison's Famous hymn, 'The spacious firmament on high', which stands in this tradition, may sound strange to modern ears, but it still has the power to move the heart as well as satisfy the mind:

What though in solemn silence all
Move round the dark terrestrial ball;
What though nor real voice nor sound
Amid their radiant orbs be found;
In reason's ear they all rejoice,
And utter forth a glorious voice,
For ever singing as thcy shine,
'The hand that made us is divine'.

Nevertheless, despite a sense of the splendor and reasonableness of God, there is little or no room in Deism for the intimate and often passionate communion of the individual heart with God which is the hallmark of much Christian piety.

Deism and similar theologies, however, commendable as they are for their honest and determined attempt to hold together scientific and religious belief, welcome as they may be for the relief which they offer to agonized questioning about why God intervenes here but not there, are in the end, I suggest, unsatisfactory.

There are weaknesses on both the scientific and the religious fronts.

Scientifically, the deistic picture is too neat and mechanical. The picture of the world as a clock, keeping to the clockmaker's time without need of any adjustment, is no longer acceptable to philosophers of science. There is indeed a massive and pervasive order in the world, or at least in those parts of it open to our study and investigation. But the order is not rigidly closed. Nor is it exactly tidy. There is an element of apparent randomness and even unpredictability in the way things go. And the more complex the system, as in an individual human being, the more room there is for novelty and even for creativity.

The more we get to know and understand the world, the less certain we become whether it does or does not point to a wise and intelligent Creator. It is so ambiguous. Sometimes it seems to suggest the presence of God, at other times the very opposite. In any case it does not appear to have been made simply and solely for the benefit of mankind, as the Deists were inclined to assume.

Religiously, the deistic picture is too optimistic. The world is a far stranger and more tragic place than Deism ever imagined to be the case. Men may aspire to be rational creatures, but they have a long way to go before they attain their goal. Sin, guilt and despair are as much part of the human scene as goodness, innocence and hope. Religion, if it is to meet man's deepest needs, has to be a religion of salvation, as well as of creation. The story of incarnation and re-demption cannot so easily be set aside as so much childish superstition.

To put the point at its sharpest: is the deistic 'God' God enough? If, having made the world, he not only lets it go and lets it be, but withdraws to his celestial observatory and abandons the world completely and ut-terly to its own devices, can we still call him by the name of boundless Love, Father of Jesus Christ? Love lets go, as we have argued. But Love draws near again — again and ever again — or it is no longer Love.

GOD'S INVOLVEMENT WITH HIS WORLD

Our deepest Christian convictions, it seems, urge us to seek some understanding of the relation of God to the world and of his way with the world which ascribes to the world a measure of real independence but does not at the same time render it God-forsaken. But how is this possible? How can we think of boundless Love as present to and in the world in such a way that the world continues to have and to exercise its own proper independence?

In the end the answer to this question is going to elude us. The relationship between Creator and creature is unique. We are not God, and we have no experience or knowledge of what it is like to be God. The only relationships of which we have any knowledge are those which occur *within* creation. We cannot get out of our creaturely skins to observe God at work. We have to admit that it is beyond our power to comprehend. Nevertheless, despite the fact that there comes a moment when we have to confess that we are in the presence of a mystery which we cannot fathom, and that the ways of God are beyond our understanding, we need not be struck completely dumb. We can make use of the theologian's stock-in-trade. We can try out various analogies. Of course, we say, God's way with the world is uniquely his own. All the same it is something like this — or, perhaps better, something like that.

Our basic faith is that the world points appealingly beyond itself, and that in Jesus Christ the Beyond has been present in our midst. In him we have been grasped by a boundless Love which invites and challenges our understanding, although it always exceeds it. We draw on analogies from our human experience in order to try to understand this most fundamental and important of all ultimate mysteries.

ANALOGIES OF GOD'S ACTION

The most obvious analogy we can use to describe the divine action is human action. God, then, acts very much as human beings act. But human action is 'embodied'. We make things happen in the world by using our bodies to make contact with other objects. We move our arms and legs, pulling here and pushing there. We intervene in the physical world around us, and we can do just this because our bodies are a part of that world.

At this point the analogy begins to break down. In fact it has never really got off the ground. God is not part of the world. He has no body such as ours. He does not 'intervene' in things in the way in which we intervene.

We could try to make the analogy work by thinking of the whole world as if it were God's body. This analogy has a long and respectable history. It is not to be despised. It reminds us that God is not another being existing alongside the world. It suggests, very helpfully, that the world is the means of God's self-communication. But its weakness is that the world, as such, does not possess the organic unity which belongs to a body. It is a multiplicity, not a unity. If it were God's body, God would surely be a pitiable schizophrenic!

Other analogies can be drawn from particular types of human activity.

A celebrated biblical analogy is that of

the potter shaping his clay. This suggests God's power to make and to destroy, but its strength is also its weakness. The analogy is too impersonal. If a potter does not like the pot he has just made, he throws it away and starts on another, with no tears shed. The pot has nothing to complain about, since it is not in the nature of pots to complain. But human beings are not pots. They are persons. And persons, however misshapen, matter. They matter most to God. So the analogy of the potter is not very satisfactory after all, despite its use by prophets and apostles such as Jeremiah (cf. Jer. ch. 18) and Paul (cf. Rom. 9:21).

We might think of the writer writing a play. The characters are his creation and have no existence apart from him, but sometimes they seem to take on a life of their own and develop their story almost independently of their author.

Or we might think of the speaker uttering his speech. He expresses his thought in his words and they acquire a certain existence and independence of their own. We could say that he puts himself into his words. Nevertheless, he remains more than his words and is not to be limited to them.

All these analogies have something to suggest to us. Some are more helpful than others. Some take us further than others. Most of them break down if they are taken too far. But this is just what we should expect. They are only analogies.

THE ANALOGY OF HUMAN LOVE

Since the mystery into which we find ourselves being drawn is the mystery of boundless Love, and since the way of God with his world as expressed and embodied in Jesus Christ is the way of Love, the most fruitful analogies will be those drawn from the realm of loving human relationships.

How do we persuade someone of our love and win their love in return, while at the same time respecting and protecting their freedom? We cannot compel, we must not manipulate. The response to love must be freely offered if it is to have the quality of love.

What we do is to *show* our love, to *be* loving. We may *do* all sorts of things. We may write poems, send flowers, mend the washing machine, cook the meals. But the things we do are not like a love-potion, calculated to produce an involuntary reaction. In a sense it does not matter what we do, so long as it is an expression and sacrament of our feelings and desires. Certainly love is active, not passive. Faint heart never won fair lady. But love finds a response more by what it *is* than by *what it does*. Love does not push, interfere, manipulate, pull the strings. Love acts by making itself present, by presenting itself *as* love. Love does all it can by arousing interest, awakening desires and winning a response.

If the way in which human love achieves its purposes throws any light on the way in which divine love achieves its purposes, then we should think less of God's compelling the world to do what he wants and more of his persuading and enabling it of its own free will to do what he wants. What this might mean at the subhuman level of atoms and organisms is and remains obscure. At the human level, however, it means that God acts through the redirection of our thoughts and desires. It is not a case of *either* God *or* man. It is a case of God in, through and together with man. In so far as our response to God is determined by our own heart and mind, rather than by an involuntary submission to his command or an unconscious reaction to his manipulation, it is our own free act. In so far as our thoughts and desires are being redirected by our recognition of God's declared love for us, they are God's own gracious gift to us. Thus God's active involvement in our lives respects and enhances our freedom. It does not destroy it.

Human beings desire many different things. Our deepest desires are the expression of what we really are, because they are made up of our hopes, our thoughts and our feelings. It is from our desires that our attitudes and our actions spring. Thus, when God presents himself to us, as he did in Jesus Christ, as the essence of Love and the supreme object of our desiring, he is not tinkering in the way the world goes about its affairs. He acts in the world by making himself present in the world. The response, when it occurs, is ours. But its beginning and its end, and the very possibility of its happening at all, lie with God.

What we have heard and seen of God in the life and person of Jesus Christ (cf. 1 John 1:1-3) lightens our darkness and engages our desire. We sense that it is the presence of his Love in the Spirit which

offers us our true and eternal identity. We
have some inkling of the workings of divine
grace. All we can know directly is the
movement of our own hearts and minds. We
have no equally direct access to the action of
God. But we have reason to believe that the
promptings of our own hearts are a response
to his Spirit within us. In Paul's paradoxical
but persuasive affirmation: 'I live; yet not I,
but Christ lives in me' (Gal. 2:20), Love
challenges and invites us and we dare to
venture a response.

At this point let us pause for a moment
and take stock of what we have been about.

In order to try to understand what we
may hope for by way of God's answer to our
prayers, we have been drawing out the impli-
cations, for our understanding of God's way
with the world, of the fact that for Christian
belief Love rather than Power is the name by
which God has made himself known.

First, neither our scientific understanding
of the world nor our Christian apprehension
of God encourages us to expect that we shall
be able to discover the hidden hand of God
at work in the world. The way that Love
works is such that it never forces itself
obviously and ostentatiously on an observer's

attention. We can never offer an altogether convincing proof that it has had any effect at all.

Second, if we believe that it is inadequate to think of God having no involvement with the world, apart from the powers which he delegated to it when he created it in the beginning, then we must suggest a way of his being involved which does justice both to our scientific and to our religious convictions.

Third, the most helpful analogies for such involvement are likely to be drawn from loving human relationships with their personal categories of freedom, responsibility and persuasion.

Fourth, such analogies help us to understand and speak about the basic mystery of God's relationship with the world, although they do nothing to dissolve it. The workings of love remain mysterious even on the human level. We should not expect them to be any the less mysterious on the divine level.

In short, we should expect the working of God's Love to make a real difference to the way that the world goes, but we should not expect to be able to detect it by scientific observation. It will work with nature rather than against it. It will evoke from nature what nature has it in herself potentially to become. It will invite and enable human beings to discover their true and full humanity as they freely respond to the vision of God which has given to them and come through their love for him to desire what is in accordance with his gracious will.

For the most part, then, we shall expect God to be active in the world by working with the grain of the world. If there are occasions when he works miracles which go against the grain of the world, how he works them and why he works them is completely beyond our understanding. We shall simply have to acknowledge their occurrence, believing that they too are the expression, albeit uncharacteristic and unfathomable, of boundless Love.

TRANSFORMATION

Since God's characteristic way with his world is to transform it from within rather than manipulate it from without, prayer cannot be a device for bypassing the reality and order of the world. It is, rather, part of that process of transformation. The believer, too, must accept the world as the context for his prayer, an ordered but open reality in which both God and man participate. Only as he himself is willing to be transformed may he pray for the world to be transformed. Only as he himself is willing to work for a new world may he pray for the coming of God's Kingdom.

In prayer the Spirit of God and the spirit of man meet and touch. The man of prayer responds to God's care and concern for the world. The faithful worshipper becomes the hopeful fellow-worker. Prayer and work are two aspects of a single response.

The believer will not expect, as a result of his prayer, that the world will now behave as if it were subject to a powerful and external manipulation. He will expect that, through his own and others' response to the Spirit of God, things will look different and, with new possibilities arising, will become different. Prayer is not a special spiritual force, but a moment in the meeting and cooperation of God and man. If prayer can move mountains, it is because Love can move mountains, the love of God kindling a fire of love within the hearts of men.

V.
ASKING, SEEKING, KNOCKING

OUR PRAYER WILL BE AS MANY-SIDED as our relationship with God. Sometimes he will seem wonderfully near to us and we shall want to sing his praises. At other times he may seem strangely absent, while the realities of the world are too much for us, and we shall want to cry out to him in protest. Sometimes we shall be deeply conscious of his graciousness and compassion, and we shall be moved to give him our humble and hearty thanks. At other times we shall be more conscious of his righteousness over against our selfishness and sin, and we shall be driven to our knees to seek his forgiveness.

Thanksgiving and praise, penitence and confessions, are clearly going to find expression in our prayers. We could not conceive of any relationship between God our Father and creatures like ourselves which did not contain these elements. But what of intercession and petition, praying for others and for ourselves? What of *asking* God for something?

ASKING

Some people think that it is wrong to ask God for anything at all. There are a number of reasons why this might be so.

Some may hold, with the Deists, that after God made the world he left it entirely to its own devices. There is no point in asking him for anything, as he does not 'do' anything. It is part of the perfection of his creation that, once it was completed in the beginning, it does not need any more to be 'done' to it. Everything that happens thereafter happens according to plan.

Others may hold that, even if God is still active in his world, asking him for this or that makes no sense, since he knows and ordains what is for the best. Asking may suggest that God will act just because we have asked him to. But what his creatures do surely cannot affect what their Creator does. He must be above and beyond all change, unmoved by prayers which we may or may not happen to make to him.

Others, again, may take what seems a highly religious line and tell us that, if only we could overcome our own desires, which express our own point of view, we should see that God is beyond everything that we call good and evil. Instead of wanting this and that we should cultivate an attitude of acceptance and indifference. A truly religious attitude, it is alleged, is one without any desires at all. Whatever happens, we should accept it.

WANTING

Wanting, it is alleged, is childish and selfish.

Those of us who were brought up on the improving moral that 'I want never got' — so very different from the Gospel preaching that those who ask get, those who seek find, and those who bang on the door loudly

enough to wake the neighbors get let in —
have been indoctrinated into thinking of
wanting as selfish. And selfish it often is, for
what I want is all too often something for
myself alone.

But what if I want the moon and the
stars for my beloved, what if I want food for
the hungry and peace for the world, what if
I want the Kingdom of God? There is
nothing necessarily selfish about wanting.
And if God has made us the sort of creatures
who are shaped by our desires, then bringing
our desires in prayer to him need be neither
selfish nor childish.

Cultivating an attitude of indifference,
pretending that we do not really mind if this
happens to us or that, acting as though it
were all the same to us because it is, sup-
posedly, all the same to God, may sound
deeply religious, but in fact it is not
Christian. Robert Capon, in *The Third
Peacock* (Image Books, New York, 1972),
puts the overwhelming objection to this kind
of submissiveness in his own inimitable Ame-
rican Style:

If you are just a common garden slob
who cries all night because they have

taken away your beloved and you know
not where they have laid him, then
frankly it looks like a sellout to a con
job: the great eternal cat lecturing the
mice on the beauties of being eaten, and
the mice lining up in the streets to fill
the hall. Once again, the only thing that
feels right is to cry out against it all like
Job: We are your creatures, dammit;
we've got *some* rights, haven't we? (p. 85).

If our very individuality is bound up with
our desires and longings, then it cannot be
true that our communion with our heavenly
Father depends upon their suppression.

Should we go far wrong if we said that
God, far from being indifferent and unmoved by his creatures, passionately longs
for their loving response and passionately
desires their greatest good? Obviously we
should be pressing a very human analogy
which cannot be taken literally. But is such
an analogy worse than that of the impersonal
and indifferent Ruler who is untouched by
the cries of his subjects? Does it not get
nearer what we have learned about God
through Jesus Christ?

It is not hard to understand why many
Christian thinkers in the past have been un-

willing to speak of God's longing. To long
for something sounds like an imperfection. It
is to lack something. But surely God has in
himself all that he needs, or he would be
something less than 'God', a Being who is
perfect by definition. To want something,
and to long for it, is therefore incompatible
with being 'God'.

There have been other Christian thinkers,
however, who have not been persuaded by
this argument. For them, perfection has con-
sisted, not in having everything, but in giving
everything. Since God is perfect Love, he
freely creates and he freely gives. There is in
God himself, as perfect Love, the perfection
of giving and receiving. And when this God
creates, he gives to his creatures sufficient
time and space in which to be themselves. He
longs for them to return his love, but he
allows them, if they so will, to reject it. He
does not compel their obedience. Thus his
longing is as much a mark of his perfection
as is his creating.

God's wanting

In the writings of Thomas Traherne, a
seventeeth-century Anglican priest and poet,

the wants of the Christian God distinguished
him from 'heathen deities' which 'wanted
nothing, and were therefore unhappy, for
they had no being'. Traherne realized that a
Love which gives itself to its creatures must
also be a love which longs for its creatures to
give themselves in return.

Traherne also made God's wants the
ground for valuing human wants: 'You must
want like God that you may be satisfied like
God. Were you not made in his image?'
There is nothing wrong with wanting as
such. Our wants, our desires, our loves lead
us, if rightly ordered, to God himself. It is a
disorder of desire that leads man away from
God. 'When we dote upon the perfections
and beauties of some one creature, we do
not love that too much, but other things too
little. Never was anything in this world loved
too much, but many things have been loved
in a false way, and all in too short a
measure.'

The image of God's love and longing,
much closer to the God of whom the Scrip-
tures bear witness than the image of an unmoved and indifferent Being above and beyond the toils and tribulations of creation,
offers a rich and fertile soil for prayer. Not

only are we drawn to praise and penitence, but we are at once invited to share in God's own love, in all his delights and desires. Nor is the movement only in one direction. God in his graciousness draws near to share in the loves and longings of his children, and gently to conform them to his own.

Desire, then, is not to be suppressed. It is to be purified, deepened and transformed. We are to learn what Love truly is and to distinguish true love from all the false 'loves' which counterfeit it. Truth and love are the pillars on which the Christian life is to be built.

'Thy kingdom come', we have been taught to pray. But this is no act of stubborn resignation. It is both the recognition of God's loving purposes for man and also the expression of a desire to participate in them. And if we really intend to want and love like God, then we must bring to our prayers ourselves as we really are — our wishes, our needs, our hopes, our fears, as well as our adoration and confession. God does not want some outwardly pious but inwardly emaciated ghost of ourselves. He wants our whole selves, our real selves. Love can be content with no less.

A merely passive 'Thy will be done' may be the expression of submission to God, but it involves a partial withdrawal of ourselves. We resign ourselves and give in to God rather than wrestle with him until day breaks (cf. Genesis 32:24). But God wants our love not merely our obedience. The Christian gospel emphasizes self-forgetfulness rather than self-suppression. There is indeed a kind of dying to self which we have to go through, but it is a death from which God has promised to raise us into a fuller life. We must let ourselves go and let God recreate us by his own Spirit.

WHAT GOD WANTS

If we are called to want like God, then we need to have some idea of what it is that God wants. Our communion with the divine demands that we should bring to our prayer our own desires and longings as they actually are, but it also demands that we should expect to have ourselves conformed by Love to the divine image and pattern. Our desires *need* not be selfish. But in fact they *are* largely selfish. We need Love's surgery and healing in order to be whole ourselves.

What, then, is it that God wants?

GOD WANTS OUR LOVE

First and foremost, he wants us to love him. This want takes precedence over everything else. It is not a matter of self-glorification, as it would be if he were only a creature. But because he is God, he alone can give us our real selves, above all that we either desire or deserve. And love is both the condition and the fulfilment of our discovering our true freedom.

God's chief care and concern are that he should be truly himself in relation to us, and that we should be truly ourselves in relation to him. This, as we have seen, is why he does not manipulate the world, but gives it the ability to make itself. He offers himself to us in and through all life's changes and chances, its agonies as well as its glories. That is the very best that he can do for us. There is nothing better that he could do. But when it comes to the agonies, God's best does not feel very good. The Christian faith is not that everything is for the best in the best of all possible worlds, but that there is nothing that can separate us from the love of God. The cross of Christ is an acknowledgment of the pain and evil in the world, and at the same time a proclamation of the unfailing love of God in the midst of it all.

In view of the fact that God does not keep intervening in the way the world goes, some have inferred that he has no care or concern for it. His love, they say, is a 'purely spiritual' love. Likewise, the love that he wants from his human creatures is said to be a 'purely spiritual' love. And they define 'spirit', not in the way in which we defined it above (cf. pp.26 -31) in terms of the personal dimension of freedom, responsibility and creativity, but in contrast and opposition to the whole material and bodily life of this world. 'Spiritual' thus comes to mean 'other-worldly'. And the bond of love between God and man comes to be one that takes man right away from his ordinary interests in the things of the world.

GOD WANTS OUR HAPPINESS

God, however, is Creator as well as Redeemer. The world is the sphere of his creativity and the object of his love. He rejoices in his creatures and desires their good.

His love for human beings, therefore, despite the limitations which it places on his intervention in the world, embraces his desire for their happiness as well as for their holiness. Just as a parent desires health and happiness for his children, even though above all else he wants them to grow into responsive and responsible adults, so God desires that his human children will flourish in all aspects of their humanity. His love is not a general but remote benevolence towards mankind; it is a love for Tom, Dick and Harry in all their individual uniqueness.

In prayer, then, we shall bring to God our varied desires for all the goods which we think will enrich our lives. Just as we are prepared to work for them, so too we shall be prepared to pray for them. Just as we have to learn what Love invites us to do and what Love forbids us to do, so too we have to learn in prayer which of our desires Love encourages and tends and which Love restrains and rebukes.

PRAYER AND ACTION

Our engagement with God will be both in prayer and in action. We are called to be his fellow-workers in making and maintaining the fabric of the world. Prayer and action are two sides of one and the same response. Praying is not a substitute for doing, nor is doing a substitute for praying.

To think we can get all the good we need through action without recourse to prayer is idolatry, since it places our own notions of what is good in the place of God. We have to learn what is really good, and it is through prayer that the learning takes place. On the other hand to turn to God without at the same time doing all that we can ourselves to bring about what we pray for is equally idolatrous. For it puts in the place of the true God, who has revealed himself in and through the way the world goes, a false god of our own imagining.

GOD WANTS US TO LOVE EACH OTHER

First and foremost, God wants us to love him; but, being the sort of God he is, he also wants us to love one another.

From God's point of view we are all his children, members of one family. We belong to one another, in the broader context as his human children, in the closer context as members of the 'Body' of Christ.

From our point of view it does not readily seem to work out like this. We are more conscious of our separateness from each other and of our conflicts with each other. A sense of isolation and alienation often seems to be stronger than a sense of community. We are a deeply divided family.

In our prayer, as in our work, the Spirit calls us to remember that through Jesus Christ we belong to one another, children of one and the same Father. Whether in the privacy of our own homes or in the midst of the congregation, we pray *'Our* Father'. We learn to pray from others. We learn to pray with others and for others.

It is God's love for all mankind which takes hold of us in prayer and broadens and deepens our love for one another — first for those with whom we have immediately to do, and then in ever widening circles for those further afield with whom God has immediately to do.

Since it is natural to pray for those whom we love, we find ourselves praying for all sorts and conditions of men. God loves them all. We are invited to love them too. Prayer for them is part of that loving. Such prayer does not take its origin from magical ideas

of getting God on one's side but from the
faith that God is already by their side.

THE COMING OF GOD'S KINGDOM

As Christians we live in a tension between
the 'already' and the 'not yet', a tension
symbolized by the imagery of the two comings of Jesus Christ. In his first coming
God's Kingdom was established on earth.
But we have still to pray for its coming,
since it is not yet here in its fullness and its
glory. So we wait and hope and work and
pray for Christ's 'second coming' at what we
call, for want of a better phrase, the 'end of
history'. We live, then, 'between the times of
the two comings'.

Our prayer, too, has the stamp of the
'between times'. There is the recognition of
what already is, the expression of joy and
confidence in the self-manifestation of God
and of his love for us. Underneath are the
everlasting arms.

At the same time there is the longing for
what is yet to be, for the remaking of heaven
and earth, for the homecoming, for the fullness of life and joy. Prayer is seeking and
searching, asking and knocking, a pilgrimage
of discovery.

It is Love which kindles hope and holds
out a promise that 'in the end' all creation
will acknowledge and respond to its Lord.
'Journeys end in lovers' meetings', but in the
meantime

> We shall not cease from exploration
> And the end of all our exploring
> Will be to arrive where we started
> And know the place for the first time.
> (T. S. Eliot, *Little Gidding*)

From God we come, to God we go, in God
we live and move and have our being.

Prayer is a sharing in God's Spirit, a
response to his self-giving Love. It is a
moment in God's continuing work of creation, redemption and consummation. It is an
exercise of man's priesthood on behalf of the
world after the manner and pattern of
Christ's eternal priesthood. It is receiving
and offering.

From prayer nothing worldly is alien.
Hopes and fears, joys and sorrows, anger
and gratitude, all provide rich material for
our prayers.

Whither shall I go then from thy
     Spirit: or whither shall I go then
     from thy presence?
If I climb up into heaven, thou art there:
     if I go down to hell, thou art there
     also.
If I take the wings of the morning: and
     remain in the uttermost parts
     of the sea;
Even there also shall thy hand lead me:
     and thy right hand shall hold me.
If I say, Peradventure the darkness shall
     cover me: then shall my night be
     turned to day.
Yea, the darkness is no darkness with
     thee, but the night is as clear as the
     day: the darkness and light to thee are
     both alike.
(Psalm 139:6-11).

There is no part of our life over which the
Spirit does not expectantly brood.

VI.
THE FRUITS OF PRAYER

THEREFORE, MY BROTHERS, I IMPLORE
you by God's mercy to offer your
very selves to him: a living sacrifice,
dedicated and fit for his acceptance, the
worship offered by mind and heart. Adapt
yourselves no longer to the pattern of this
present world, but let your minds be remade
and your whole nature thus transformed.
Then you will be able to discern the will of
God, and to know what is good, acceptable,
and perfect' (Romans 12:1-2 NEB).

Prayer in Context

All our thinking about Christian prayer, whether and how it works, what difference it makes, its value and its validity, must keep firmly in mind the context in which it occurs. This context is the union of divine and human love, the double movement of God to man and of man to God. The nature of this union is so important that it is worth drawing attention again to its main characteristics.

This union was realized in Jesus Christ and continues to make itself real 'through' Jesus Christ 'in' the Spirit among those who are 'members' of his 'body'.

The special promise and pledge of this continuing movement is the sacrament of Holy Communion, the ritual representation of love's creative and redemptive work.

When in the sacrament we plead the sacrifice of Christ and in union with him offer ourselves to God, the whole of that process is a giving and receiving in one. It might indeed be urged that the receiving is *prior* to the giving, because the initiative is always with God and the response is ours. Yet it can hardly be said that there is a *temporal* sequence. The very giving of ourselves to God is a receiving of Him, and the very receiving of Him is already a giving of ourselves. (Donald M. Baillie, *The Theology of the Sacraments* [Faber and Faber 1957], p. 122)

All Christian prayer participates in this movement of giving and receiving and so gives form and direction to life and work.

In our prayer we offer God our worship and praise and thanksgiving. We also bring to him our longings and our desires as part of our offering and service. They are for Love to accept, purify and transform, so that we may become instruments of the divine will.

So Love knits together prayer and action into a unity of service. Just as Jesus called his disciples both to be with him and to be sent forth, so his Spirit continues to call to communion and cooperation, 'a living sacrifice'.

To take prayer out of this context of the union of divine and human love, and to ask whether God 'answers' our prayers in exactly the same sense as one human being may answer another human being's request for fresh air by getting up out of the chair and opening the window, is to forget that God is the Creator and not part of the world. As we have seen, his way with the world is not to manipulate it by pulling hidden strings but to inspire and to enable it, while maintaining its own initiative, to reach out for the gifts which he alone can give.

GETTING ANSWERS

To look for 'answers' to our petitions in a literal, anthropomorphic and simple way in order to prove that prayer 'works' is to land oneself in a quandary.

There will always be those who will give their assured testimony that, when they have prayed, God has time and time again granted their requests. What they have prayed for has come to pass. Such testimony can be impressive.

On the other hand, there is the equally striking, if often silent, testimony of those who have made their requests to God to no seeming avail, the world continuing along the same relentless way as before.

What are we to make of this conflicting testimony?

There can be no controlled tests to discover whether prayer actually 'works', or whether it is only a matter of chance. Controlled tests are essentially manipulative. They seek to bypass personal considerations. Put love to that sort of test and it flies out of the window.

Appeals to experience, therefore, must depend not only on what actually happens, but also on the underlying attitudes, expectations and interpretations of those involved. It is these latter which we have been sifting. They depend entirely on what sort of God we believe in and how this God works in his world.

We have argued that the answers to both these questions must be given in terms of creative and redemptive Love and of the categories which such Love shows to be appropriate.

THE CONTEXT OF A LOVING RELATIONSHIP

If love provides us with the necessary context and categories for understanding prayer, then clearly it cannot be the case that we should view prayer merely as a means of getting what we want. Nevertheless, although we go wrong if we concentrate on 'getting results' from prayer, this does not mean that prayer has no results, or that God never 'answers' prayer at all. We may hesitate to point to this or that occurrence in the world as God's answer to our particular petition. We may prefer to be as cautious in our claims as Archbishop William Temple, who is reported to have said: 'When I pray, coincidences happen'. But we still confidently expect prayer to have its own ample fruits, since the activity of the Spirit cannot prove barren. In John Burnaby's words (in *Soundings,* ed. A. R. Vidler [CUP 1962]): ' "What happens when I pray" is, to begin with, an encroachment of the love of God on the defenses of my self, my hard heart and laggard will. But it is not possible that the effect of such encroachment should be confined to the place where it has been made' (p. 232-3).

What, then, are the fruits of prayer?

TRANSFORMATION AND TRANSFIGURATION

First, there is a kind of transfiguration, the discovery of the presence of the divine within the ordinary.

Prayer itself is a response to God's special presence in the here-and-now to the one who is praying. God comes. He already prays with us and for us. As we respond, not only are we ourselves in process of transformation, but the world in which we are living is also transfigured for us.

Picturesquely, such transfiguration is expressed in the story of Elisha, who prayed that God would open the eyes of his young serving-lad, who was terrified by the surrounding armies of the enemy. His eyes were indeed opened, and he saw 'horses and chariots of fire' on the mountainside (cf. 2 Kings 6:8-17). Less picturesquely but just as strikingly, our own situations can be totally transfigured in the light of the cross of Jesus Christ and of his risen presence. Ordinary bread and wine become his Body and Blood. He himself is with us, and our world takes on a different significance in his presence.

The world is transfigured and our hearts and minds are transformed. So God gives not only himself, the greatest gift of all, but also his special help in our time of need.

There are two kinds of help that one person may give to another. There is, on the one hand, the helping hand. If I am too ill to go to the shops myself to get some food for the weekend, a good neighbor will often go for me. This is the most practical help that he can give. Often it is what I most need.

On the other hand there is what we might call the helping spirit. What I may need more than anything else is someone by me and with me, someone to listen and to share with me. He may do nothing. There may be nothing practical that he can do. But I know that I could not have got by without the help and strength I received from his presence. 'But I did nothing!', he may exclaim, when at some later date I offer him my halting thanks. However, it was not what he did or did not do. It was what he was, and the fact he made himself available to me at that time, that proved the difference for me between life and death.

We can, I think, best understand God's concrete and personal help in answer to our prayers along lines such as these. And maybe that is enough. It certainly fits in with all that we were saying earlier about God's way with the world. It provides a firm basis for petition as well as for contemplation. And it eliminates all those puzzles about God's doing and not doing which both science and ordinary experience raise and which disturb our faith.

If, as is sometimes said, Christ has no hands but our hands, then God achieves his purposes in the world, first, by sending Jesus as the Christ, and now by sending us in the name of Jesus Christ. It all depends on us, and we depend on God.

SPECIAL PROVIDENCE?

Is it possible, all the same, to think of ways in which boundless Love could shape the world of human history apart from the wills and actions of men in whom that love has come to dwell?

The principle which we put forward earlier was that the way of Love was not to intervene in the world by pushing here and pulling there, but to invite its creatures to be more fully themselves as they respond to Love's invitation.

Now it may be the case that the natural world is more complex and more open than we ordinarily assume, and that the network of causal connections is less restricted than we imagine. If so, it may be that prayer brings into play a wider causality than usual and that this becomes available for the service of Love.

For example, there may be links and connections between human beings at the psychological, and even at the unconscious, as well as at the physical level. The evidence for telepathy, if uncertain, is at least sufficiently impressive to be taken seriously.

If these connections do in fact exist, then what we can 'do' for others in response to the gentle but insistent pressure of the divine love is not restricted to our ordinary physical actions. These latter are sometimes undoubtedly the fruits of prayer. They flow from the decisions which we make as a consequence of our prayers. But we may also be 'doing' something for others in the very act of prayer itself. We may be making resources available for them which stem directly from our praying and which they are able to use themselves.

Telepathy, if it occurs, is as much a part

of the natural world as are more usual forms of communication. Hence, if prayer for others establishes a telepathic link with them, this in itself is no proof that God has 'intervened' in the course of the world and so has 'answered' prayer. If the telepathic link is the expression of the union between divine and human love, then it may properly be called the fruit of prayer.

MIRACLES?

If God works with the world rather than in spite of the world, then in principle he may be responsible for anything which is in accord with the nature and purposes of Love and the structures and potentialities of the world. Because our knowledge and understanding of both are limited, we cannot draw clear boundaries around what God can and cannot do. We must preserve a certain openness of mind. And because it is in the nature of Love to do more than we either desire or deserve, working wonders beyond our expectation, we may pray eagerly in hope as well as confidently in faith.

The prayer of love works 'miracles'. But what of miracles, in the more precise sense of the word? Does God ever act against, rather than with, the natural order of the world?

This is obviously not the place in which to undertake a detailed discussion of the miraculous in Christian belief. But a few points may be appropriate.

In principle there is nothing to be said against the idea that God, who is the Creator of the world, should on occasion dispense with the order which he has created. Such a dispensation would not be a lapse into anarchy, but would be part of a larger and more inclusive order and design which God alone can encompass.

Furthermore, Christian tradition has not been loath to ascribe such miracles to God in answer to the prayers of his people. Jesus himself, the Gospels testify, worked a number of miracles and his disciples continue to exercise such power in his name. Things still occur from time to time for which we have no other explanation.

On the other hand, the whole thrust of our argument concerning God's way with the world has been to stress the relative independence which God has granted the world and the limitations which his being as Love places on him in his dealings with it. It is along lines such as these that we have attempted to find some answer to the question 'If God can work miracles, why does he work so few?'. It may be that some other more satisfactory answer will be forthcoming. Until then we must choose between the sort of answer that we have attempted and an acceptance of the tradition despite our total and often agonized lack of understanding. In neither case can we dispense with faith. In both cases we may be sure that God can be trusted to do all that Love can do.

Fortunately we do not have to solve the theoretical question concerning the miraculous before we get on with the business of praying.

Our hopes and wishes

We can bring to God in prayer our wishes and dreams as well as our more sober hopes and expectations. Our confidence does not lie in our getting our applications convincing and correct, but in his doing all that he can for good as we offer ourselves, our hearts and minds, to him.

Of course, the balance of wishes and hopes will vary from individual to individual, as well as in the same individual at different stages of life's pilgrimage. Our desires and our expectations change as we change. What once occupied the center of our attention may now have moved to the circumference. What we once dismissed from our minds as childish may now have acquired a special significance for us. And all these changes we can confidently share with God, and in so sharing receive the gifts that he has to give us.

PRAYER AND CHANGE

Change is the fruit of faith, discipleship and prayer. Change may be sudden or gradual, or, more probably, both. There will be special turning points and also a continuing process of growth. The Christian disciple who shares with his fellow Christians in common prayer, and also wrestles with God in the secret places of his own heart, may expect change and welcome it. He will be ready for his mind to be remade and his nature transformed. At the same time he will find that his world also is changing. It is now perceived to be under the lordship of God, an adventure of divine Love and the workshop of eternity. New tasks are revealed, new potentialities realized. The world is transfigured in the light of God's coming Kingdom. Both world and Kingdom provide us with rich material for prayer. We hold together before God past and future, time and eternity. Open to his Spirit we make room for his continuing activity in the world. The fruit of prayer is the fruit of the Spirit.

VII.
NEW BEGINNINGS

DOES GOD ANSWER PRAYER?'
The question now no longer seems quite the same question as it was when we began to consider it.

In one sense, it has become a simpler question and can be given a simple answer. Of course God answers prayer. It is his Spirit which moves us to prayer in the first place. Furthermore, he is more ready to hear than we are to pray, and he wishes to give more than we either desire or deserve.

In another sense, the question has become more complex. We can be assured that God has not abandoned his world but continues to act in it. Nevertheless, we cannot know for certain how or where his activity occurs. For the most part it remains hidden, working with and through natural causes. Above all, it works in and through the hearts and minds of his human creatures. We become his fellow workers in the Spirit.

Our prayers will change as we change. There is no single blueprint for praying to our Father. We begin by praying as we can, not as we believe that we ought. Our prayers will be varied and flexible, the expression of our true selves. That is the service which God asks from us.

Books about prayer may have their uses but they are no substitute for prayer itself.

There is an art of praying, and it takes time to learn. There is a discipline as well as a spontaneity. But the learning can itself be part of the praying, and the finding can be in the seeking.

You do not have to be an expert in spiritual communication in order to respond to the Spirit of God. Few of us can become experts in prayer. For this reason we need never be too proud to learn from one another. We can draw upon the prayers of the Church, the prayers of the Bible, and the prayers of individuals, ancient and modern.

These prayers we shall want to make our own, or adapt to our own needs. Some will find an echo in our hearts more easily than others. Others will simply not be for us.

Nor need we be ashamed of our own faltering prayers, even if they amount to not much more than, 'I love you'. If our prayer is true, what more needs to be said? And there is always the prayer of silence, just being with God.

Prayer begins and ends with God, his longing for us and our longing for him. A sense and conviction that Love beckons to us is the kindling of that longing.

Let the seventeenth-century poet George Herbert provide us with an end which may also be a beginning.

Love bade me welcome: yet my soul drew
    back
        Guiltie of dust and sinne.
But quick-ey'd Love, observing me grow
    slack
        From my first entrance in,
Drew nearer to me, sweetly questioning,
        If I lack'd any thing.

A guest, I answer'd, worthy to be here:
   Love said, You shall be he.
I the únkinde, ungrateful? Ah my deare,
   I cannot look on thee.
Love took my hand, and smiling did
   reply,
      Who made the eyes but I?

Truth Lord, but I have marr'd them: let
   my shame
      Go where it doth deserve.
And know you not, sayes Love, who bore
   the blame?
      My deare, then I will serve.
You must sit down, sayes Love, and taste
   my meat:
      So I did sit and eat.

122